SCRIPTWRITING AND STRUCTURE

SCRIPTWRITING AND STRUCTURE

Anthony Herron

iUniverse, Inc.
New York Lincoln Shanghai

SCRIPTWRITING AND STRUCTURE

iUniverse books may be ordered through booksellers or by contacting:

iUniverse
2021 Pine Lake Road, Suite 100
Lincoln, NE 68512
www.iuniverse.com
1-800-Authors (1-800-288-4677)

ISBN: 0-595-34627-8

Printed in the United States of America

Contents

ACKNOWLEDGMENTS

Susan: Thank you for being my loving and wonderful wife.

Sidney Poitier: Thank you for giving me my first writing break.

John Truby: You are the master, the sage, the authority of scriptwriting instruction. Thank you for providing me with the knowledge and inspiration to write this book.

David Margolis: Thank you for being the first person, on your level, to teach me scriptwriting. Thank you for your guidance and your friendship through all of these years.

Daniel "Rudy" Ruettiger: Your positivity and tenacity is infectious.

Chad Hoffman: Taking the time to help me is appreciated.

Josh Donen: Thanks for being so cool to me.

Professor Charles Deemer: You are a scriptwriting guru. Thank you for all of your help.

Tony Brown: Your work in the "community" is greatly appreciated and inspiring.

Van: You are still my "chief counseler" and I appreciate you.

Willard Pugh: Thank you "Harpo" for all of your help and input in my journey toward being a better scriptwriter and overall better person.

Erick Benson: Thank you, writing partner, for being the great person and writer that you are.

Ken Dixon: You are a good friend and I admire your great attitude; thank you for sharing.

Susan Garrison: Thank you for all of your help at Verdun-Cedric.

INTRODUCTION

This book is intended to instruct anyone, from a person that has an idea for a movie to a seasoned writer. Its primary purpose is to instruct you on how to properly structure your script. This book is written in a vertical, airy form that is easy to read and understand. It is intentionally a short book that is focused on Structure and the Main Character. Everything that concerns the Main Character is covered here including his dialogue, his "friends", his Opponent and his "friends" and where his actions take place. Actually, these elements comprise the whole script.

The terms "main character" and "hero" are use interchangeably; they are one in the same. They are intentionally interchanged, sometimes within the same sentence, so that consciously and subconsciously, you will use them interchangeably. The term protagonist and antagonist are not used in order to dispel any thought that the main character/hero is necessarily a good person and the Opponent (so-called villain/bad guy) is a bad person. The main character/hero could be a "bad" person and the Opponent could be a good guy. In The Terminator (the first one), the Terminator is the main character/hero but he is a bad guy.

The terms "he", "his" and "him" do not refer to a male; this term is used in the neuter gender and can be applied to a female as well. These terms are used only to prevent writing he/she, his/her, him/her or having to explain in every instance that a particular pronoun could be either male or female. Therefore, each time a character is referred to as "he", "him" or "his", its reference is to a male or female.

The first letter of a word of a particular subject is capitalized to emphasize the use of that particular word in the sentence. For instance, because genre is one of the subjects that is covered, each time the word Genre appears, it is capitalized.

There are many different aspects of scriptwriting that are not covered in this book. There are many scriptwriting books that cover many, varied detailed aspects of the scriptwriting process.
These books cover everything from the font of the script, to how to market it, to the various software to use. In this information age that includes the internet, there is an endless amount of information on practically any subject under the sun, including scriptwriting.

However, there is little or no information in most of those references on Structure, especially to the depth and detail that Structure is covered in this book. Combine your story and your creativity with the elements of this book and Structure your ideas into a great script.

SCRIPTBUILDING AND STORY STRUCTURE

Almost everyone has an idea for a movie but very few know how to properly write a script. This book will not make your story good but it will help to turn a good story into a good script. This book cannot teach you creativity but it can help you to structure your creative ideas into a great script form.

A script must be STRUCTURED so that it will be cohesive; that it will stay together. The Classic Structure is the framework of the script. Script building or building a script through structure is analogous to the structure of a human being. The human body is composed of many different systems such as the digestive, lymphatic, circulatory, nervous, respiratory and muscular. All of these systems are essential to the make-up of the human system. However, these systems cannot "stand" without the skeletal system, within which all of the various systems are "wrapped around" and/or "encased". Without the "structure" of the skeletal system, the human body would "fall" apart. Without structure in the scriptwriting process, the story will fall apart. Just as "the thigh bone is connected to the knee bone," etc. then the key to structure is linkage; linking each part of the story so that no part "hangs" by itself. This is the reason that so many stories/movies fall apart. This is why they have "slow" and boring parts. The classic structure will make your script/story so strong that it **will not** have slow or boring parts and it will not fall apart. The characters and scenes will be fully developed.

Structure is needed in order to be able to explain the story, especially in telling stories about humans. Since humans are complex, then telling stories about human beings are complex. All good scripts have the same basic structure. For instance, *The Karate Kid* and *Jerry Maguire* have common elements in that Daniel is the only student of Mr. Miyagi and Rod Tidwell is the only client of Jerry Maguire. *Rocky, The Karate Kid* and *Titanic* are all basically Love Stories. The assassin in *The Professional,* Susan Sarandon's character in *Stepmom* and Denzel Washington's character in *Man on Fire* all have the same caring nature for the children in their lives.

Structure is the order of what your main character does; the order of your main character's development; the order of scenes. Structure tells what the story is. It is the single largest pattern and organizer in the story. Your Structure can be organized and manipulated and changed. If you need to change your story of these things, go to the structure first, not the dialogue.

The terms that are introduced here will be terms and concepts that are easily and readily applied. There is a lot of writing terminology that is quite familiar in writing circles and are generally known by the masses. Terms like: conflict; progressive complications; climax; resolutions are readily recognized, but applying them to your character and in your story can be difficult. Where do they apply? How and where do they fit? The terms used in the Classic Structure herein will be a methodology that will have practical, definable terms that can be easily and readily applied. All good scripts contain the Classic Structure.

NOTES

THE 7-STEP STORY STRUCTURE

There are seven basic, yet major steps in the Classic Structure. These seven steps are the skeleton of your script that holds your script together. These steps exemplify how human nature works. This is breaking up human action into steps and anyone who has a lack and/or need will go thru these steps in order to get what they want. These steps will help you write a good story. You can apply these steps to any story, any movie and almost any human endeavor because this is the way human beings act. Let's use the *Wizard of Oz* as a template for the examples of each of the steps of the structure.

1. PROBLEM/NEED

This is the difficulty of the main character from the beginning of the story. He is aware of the Problem but he does not know the solution. The Problem is something **external**.

EXAMPLE:
Dorothy thought that she was not appreciated and that by running away she would have a happier life.

NEED
This is something that is missing from **within** the character that must be fulfilled for a better life. The need is/should be something positive because it is this need that must be fulfilled in order for the main character to have a more meaningful, fulfilling life.

EXAMPLE:
Dorothy needed to appreciate those around her and understand that they loved her and sincerely cared about her.

THE INCITING INCIDENT

This is a major outside event that causes the main character to form a GOAL & TAKE ACTION. This is a very powerful event that happens to the main character that forces the general Desire of the main character to become VERY SPECIFIC. The Inciting Incident must be a major event; it must be a very strong, powerful event because it is this event that will force the main character to form his Goal (Desire). The Inciting Incident is a major weight on the main character but it is also an opportunity for him to move to a higher stage, deal with life and fulfill his Need.

Because most humans have the same basic Desires in life, the Inciting Incident does not have to be something that is particularly unique; therefore, there is no need to try to think of something new or creative. However, it must be something powerful enough to drive the main character to pursue his goal throughout the entire course of the story.
Only upon the achievement of his Goal (or loss of his goal) will the main character end this pursuit of this Goal, thereby ending your story.

EXAMPLE:
Dorothy's best friend, Toto, was threatened with being taken away so she needed to run away to protect Toto.

2. DESIRE

This is the GOAL that the main character has to fulfill. This Desire/Goal must be very strong, intense and specific. This is the track of which your entire story will run. There is a difference between the Need and the Desire: A lion hasn't eaten in 3 days; it sees a zebra; it has a **desire** to eat; this will fulfill the **need** of being hungry.

In *Flashdance,* the main character has a Need to be a dancer; to express herself artistically. Her Desire is to be accepted in the ballet school and to dance for the ballet.

In good stories, the Need is a moral need; that is, the main character has to learn how to act toward other people. He starts out acting toward other people in an improper way and needs to grow. The main character is aware of his moral need; however, you as the writer must know the Need of the main character in the beginning.

EXAMPLE:
Dorothy had various layers of very strong desires. She first ran away from home to escape Miss Gulch's threat to take Toto. While Dorothy was visiting Professor Marvel, a storm brewed and Dorothy wanted to go back home. After Dorothy arrived in Munchkinland she was hailed as a heroine for killing the Wicked Witch of the East. The sister of the dead witch that Dorothy had killed, the Wicked Witch of the West threatened Dorothy, "I'll get you my pretty and your little dog, too." Being threatened by a wicked witch, a witch that Glenda the Good Witch said is worse than the first, is a very powerful Inciting Incident that causes Dorothy to want to go back home to Kansas. Glenda tells Dorothy that the powerful Wizard of Oz will help her get back to Kansas. The Wizard lives in Oz and Dorothy's DESIRE is to get to Oz, see the Wizard and then hopefully, go back home.

ALLY

This is the sounding board of the main character. There may be one or more than one. The ally hears the values and the Plan of the main character. Do not write your ally to be a "spit-bucket carrier" of the main character. No disrespect intended but no one cares about the person that carries the spit bucket of the boxing champion. Do not have an ally that is just a lackey or yes-man to your main character. Develop a Desire line for the ally. This must be done quickly, without stopping or taking away for the on-going story. A quick, easy way to give an ally a Desire line is to give the ally the same or similar Desire line that the main character has.

EXAMPLE:
On the way to Oz to see the Wizard, Dorothy meets three allies (the Scarecrow; the Tin Man; the Cowardly Lion) that need something that a wizard might possibly be able to help them with. Therefore, the main character and the allies all have a similar goal.

TALISMAN

This is something possessed by the main character to help him toward the goal. It cannot make him invincible, especially to the opponent. Example: Ruby Slippers; a sword; a gun; a necklace.

The Ruby Slippers were a sort of talisman in that Glenda told Dorothy" to "keep tightly in them; they must have magical powers or the Witch wouldn't want them so badly".

3. THE OPPONENT

This is the one that prevents the main character from reaching his Goal. The Opponent is not just a block. Like the main character, the Opponent has a strong Desire, which brings on direct conflict. The Opponent causes the main character to grow and drives the main character to greatness.

These are primary characteristics of a good Opponent:

1) The opponent is necessary to the main character.
2) He is the one person in the world that is most able to attack the main character's great weakness.
3) He is human in nature and he is primarily in the same place as the main character.
4) He must want generally the same thing that the Main character wants; they must compete for generally the same thing.
5) He forces the main character to overcome his weakness or be destroyed; then the opponent forces the main character to confront his weakness and overcome it.
6) The opponent has his own beliefs and values that oppose the beliefs and values of the main character.

There are the 3 types of opponents:

1. Human: This opponent is not necessarily a good person but he does exhibit human characteristics.
Examples: Apollo Creed in *Rocky*; Sgt. Foley in *An Officer and a Gentleman*
2. Animal: This opponent's key motivation is survival. Like an animal, his actions are primarily committed by what he perceives as necessary to his survival and/or attainment of his goals. What he does and why he does them are primarily out of his need to survive. If he does something bad, it is

not because he is necessarily evil but it is because he feels that what he is doing is mainly necessary for him to win and/or survive. For example, humans greatly fear sharks. Farmers see foxes as a menace because foxes eat chickens and sheep. Neither sharks nor foxes are inherently evil; they both kill and eat in order to survive.

Examples: Don Corleone in *The Godfather*; Belloq in *Raiders of the Lost Ark*; Scarface; Apollo Creed can be viewed as both a human and an animal opponent. He beats Rocky as vehemently as possible, not because he is evil but because beating one's opponent is what a boxer must do in order to win the bout.

3. Machine: An opponent that does evil primarily for the sake of doing evil. This opponent does evil without emotion or compunction.

Examples: The Wicked Witch in the *Wizard of Oz*; Drago in *Rocky IV*; the opponents of *The Terminator 2 & 3*.

EXAMPLE:

The Wicked Witch of the West is the Opponent and she has allies as well. The witch's Desire and Dorothy's Desire are different. However, since Glenda told Dorothy to keep tightly within the ruby slippers and that they must have magical powers, Dorothy is not going to take them off. When the witch tells Dorothy that the ruby slippers cannot be removed as long as Dorothy is alive, this brings the main character and the Opponent into direct conflict.

4. THE PLAN

The Plan is "How to do what." This plan must be precise. The Plan is the main character's blueprint, road map and scheme that he will follow in order to reach his Goal. Sometimes there is some TRAINING involved for the main character. That is, he has to learn about something or learn how to do something in order to reach his goal. The Training process is more prevalent in action and sports stories; however, training is used in other story types as well. For instance, a robber may have to train to climb a rope or to crack a safe in a specified time. To overcome the opponent, the main character must come up with a PLAN of action. In all stories the main character has some sort of plan.

EXAMPLE:
Dorothy's Plan was very simple, to "Follow the yellow brick road."

APPARENT DEFEAT

This is the lowest point of the main character. He feels that he has lost but he subconsciously employs the adage that whatever doesn't kill him will strengthen him.

Dorothy is apparently defeated when she is captive in the witch's dungeon. She sinks so low that she tells the witch that she can have the ruby slippers.

5. THE BATTLE

This decides who wins: the main character or the Opponent. This is a fight between the main character and the Opponent that brings about a convergence of action, character and space. The main character fulfills his Desire here. This is also the place where the main character is most similar to his Opponent. The Battle is very intense and it tests the character. The Main character and the Opponent come into conflict in trying to reach the Goal. The Battle is the final confrontation which decides who is going to get the Goal. In the act of the Battle (which is a CRUCIBLE) there is a major test, which brings about a change. In the Battle, the main character has a major Self-Revelation.

EXAMPLE:
Dorothy and her allies have a Battle in the witch's castle that leads to the witch lighting the Scarecrow on fire. Dorothy, in her attempt to help the Scarecrow, throws water on the witch. The water melts the witch and Dorothy wins the Battle and gets the witch's broom. Getting the broom was Dorothy's goal because the Wizard told her that if she brought him the broom he would grant Dorothy her wish (Goal).

6. SELF-REVELATION

The most active and courageous act in the entire story is when the main character gets a big revelation of who he really is. The main character has a shattering moment where the façade that he has lived in is stripped away. He learns how to act properly toward others. This shows the audience how the main character has undergone change and it is directly tied to his Problem/Need. This Self-Revelation fulfills the original need. The main character is a changed/better person and has moved to a higher stage. The Self-Revelation is a key point because we are concerned with how the main character has changed by going thru the crucible of the Battle.

EXAMPLE:
After the Wizard leaves in his balloon without Dorothy, Glenda appears and tells Dorothy that she had the ability to go home anytime that she wanted to. The Scarecrow asks Glenda why she did not tell Dorothy this. Glenda replied, "She had to learn this on her own". When Dorothy is asked what did she learn, Dorothy replied that if she ever wanted have an adventure that she only needed to go as far as her own back yard.

7. NEW EQUILIBRIUM

All is back to normal. The main character has moved to either a higher (positive; stronger) level or lower (negative; bad) level.

EXAMPLE:
Dorothy is finally happily back home again and declares, "There's no place like home".

APPLYING AND LINKING THE STRUCTURE POINTS

Use Structure as a powerful tool on which you construct your story by applying the following steps:

1. Make sure your story hits the steps of the Classic Structure.
2. Present a strong moral argument.
3. Present a worthwhile problem and actually solve it.
4. Give your main character a personal problem but also a bigger, more universal problem.
5. Link each step of the Classic Structure. Each event must be linked to what came before with what comes afterward. Employ all of the points of the Classic Structure and link them together logically and progressively.

NOTES

DEVELOPING A PREMISE LINE

Many writers, even good writers, encounter many problems in creating their story.

1. Some writers think the plot is different from the character.
The plot is what the main character does over the course of the story.
The character is defined by his actions over the course of the story.

2. Some writers think that action is the same as the plot. Action is not the plot; action can kill the plot. Plot occurs with change of action when the main character does something **essentially different.**

A good premise line is stating the story in one line. State the main character, the Inciting Incident and the outcome of the story all in one line. Formulating a good premise line is the most important decision in writing a good script.

These instructions are good guides to help you create your premise line and develop your story.

1. KNOW YOUR ENDING: From the beginning, know how to solve the Problem and how to fulfill the Need of the Main character. In fact, you should know all of the structural elements of your script, in the BEGINNING of the story.
2. Central Conflict: Determine who fights whom about what. This determines a true premise line. Example: In the Karate Kid, in spite of being injured, Daniel fights for his personal dignity. He tells Mr. Miyagi that if he doesn't fight, "They will think that they got the best of me." He also says that he is fighting so that he can have balance with himself and Ali.

3. Present a strong moral argument.
4. Make sure that you solve a worthwhile problem.
5. Try to write something that may change your life. What you would like to see on the screen.
6. Make sure that your story includes all of the structural steps.
7. Figure out the central moral choice/decision. This determines the theme. Create your story so that the main character must choose between two positives (not a positive and a negative).

Example: In *The Karate Kid*: Daniel chooses to fight for honor instead of revenge.

Choice: Love or Honor. Make choice difficult and as close as possible.

In *An Officer and a Gentleman*, Mayo chooses to help a fellow recruit rather than set a record.

8. Develop a story and answer this question: Is this story interesting to others? Be extremely critical in answering this question.

NOTES

MAKE THE AUDIENCE CARE ABOUT YOUR STORY

Presenting a good Moral Argument will draw an audience into your story of which they may agree or disagree with your point of view. To make the audience agree with your point of view is not your goal but what is of utmost importance is that you present your view in a way that the audience will take interest in it and possibly relate to it. This is what happens when people are discussing what should have happened or what a character should have done or how much they liked or disliked the actions of a character or characters in particular movies. They are presenting their own moral argument.

Your Moral Argument is expressing your view of the way that a person should act/behave in the world. This is an argument of action.

For instance, your main character has a Goal; then the Opponent has the same Goal. Your main character begins to lose to the Opponent and now does immoral things in order to win. He gets criticized by his Ally and defends himself. Many times he will criticize himself in the Battle. In his Self-Revelation, he realizes that he made some bad decisions at which time the Moral Argument is established and confirmed. It is based on the main character's actions of right and wrong in the pursuit of his Goal.

One of the manifestations of a great character is that they always deal in human situations. Audiences, the general public, identify with and empathize with these situations because these situations are very real in the life of every human being. Everyone desires something and they do something, good and/or bad to get what they want. After the thing desired is attained, if the person did something that they consider wrong or bad to attain their goal, they may have remorse for their actions and maybe even modify their way of thinking and behaving presently and in the future.

"Good" character is subjective of which what is good or bad for one may not be so for another. Even still, the argument of what is good or bad is of enough interest for someone to at least debate and maybe even defend one or the other side. A debate and defense of what was right or wrong about your character's action in a particular situation is the precise intention of the Moral Argument that you created because the audience cares about your story.

To further make the audience emotionally connect with the story and with the MAIN CHARACTER, give the MAIN CHARACTER something that the audience can relate to and/or empathize with. In the Classic Structure, this is achieved through the Ghost/Problem/Need and Desire. These elements of the Classic Structure are the ones that the audience will relate to most. Everyone has some Problem, Need and Desire in their life.

There are many topics that immediately grab the attention of people and that conjure up strong feelings within people:
Politics
Religion
Sports: Who is the best team ever; who is the best at a certain position, etc.
Music: Who was the best group of a certain era; the best singer, guitarist, etc of a certain era.
TV and Movies: What was the best TV show/movie in a certain era and or within a certain genre.

GHOST

Ghost is the event from the past that still haunts the main character in the present. This is the Problem of the Main character before page 1; the Problem that is haunting the hero before the story starts. Ghost is the source of the main character's Need/great weakness and his great fear. It is what is lacking in the main character. Ghost is the internal opponent of the main character and it hinders him from going after his Desire. The hero's external opposition is, of course, the Opponent.

In *The Wizard of Oz*, Dorothy didn't feel appreciated and she felt the need to go to distant places in order to have a full life. She felt that she needed to get away.
In *The Karate Kid*, Daniel's Ghost was that he was the only child of a single parent and had been transplanted from New Jersey to California. He did not have any truly intimate relationships.

Ghost is very important in that it gives your story a running start and makes your story interesting. It causes Need and Need is the beginning line of the whole story.

BACKSTORY

Before page one of your script, something has already happened to the hero.
Usually, the Backstory is not seen by the audience but it is there, affecting the actions of the main character. In comparing Ghost to the Backstory, many times, the Backstory is a much broader, more general term. Ghost is what haunts the main character that causes his NEED. The Backstory is simply a past occurrence. Backstory is not in every story, neither is it necessary.

In The Karate Kid, Daniel's Backstory was that he did not learn karate in a real dojo. He did not know how to stand up for himself and didn't know how to handle himself. He had no real discipline.

NOTES

MAKING THE MAIN CHARACTER MORE INTERESTING

✦

DEVELOPING THE MAIN CHARACTER

As much as possible, make your main character interesting and exciting. He will be more interesting if the audience can identify with him. This does not mean that the audience must identify with superficial aspects of the main character's background, job, dress, race, gender or economic condition. Your story will be more powerful if the audience identifies with the moral problem and the desire of the main character. The audience does not necessarily have to like the main character but write your story so that the audience empathizes with him. The main character may become unlikable in his attempt to win, but if the audience understands or relates to the main character's actions, they may not like him but their empathizing with him makes your story stronger. To further strengthen your story, give your main character a moral and psychological need. This moral need involves your main character's learning how to properly act towards others. This has an effect on others and causes the audience to connect with him. In love stories, one character has a psychological need to find love; his moral need is learning how to love. In The Verdict, Paul Newman's character, Frank Galvin, has a psychological need to stop drinking; his moral need is to get respect and become a respected lawyer.

To develop and strengthen your main character, do not allow your main character to become "stupid", as in the stereotypical horror stories. This brings a mechanical contrivance to your story of which your audience will readily recognize and which will render your story and your main character's actions, unbelievable. Therefore, avoid anything that prevents your main character from making a free choice. To prevent your story and your main character from being too limited, avoid giving him a disease or addiction. This reduces your main character to a victim of which this limited story usually stirs up either repulsion or pity for this character. Though Nicholas Cage did win a Best Actor Oscar for Leaving Las Vegas, his character was very limited. An actor's performance may be great but the characters in these stories are usually repulsive. Val Kilmer was great in The Doors and Meg Ryan was great in When a Man Loves a Woman but again these characters were limited. Again, as in horror stories, avoid making your main character psychotic or insane; this reduces your main character to a monster of which few will relate to him or empathize with him. An example of a character that was fearsome but was still an interesting character is Darth Vader. Though Darth Vader in Star Wars was very much a feared character, (he was not the main character) he was feared, but he was neither psychotic nor insane. The Terminator was so well developed that even he became a likeable and empathetic character. The process of developing your main character is made more powerful by giving him a Range of Change.

RANGE OF CHANGE

This is the range of which the main character can change or grow over the course of the story. Make this possible at beginning of the story. Be sure to give your character a wide Range of Change because the broader the range of change, the more interesting the story will be. Range of Change is character development; the changes of the basic beliefs of the main character to take new moral action.

These are NOT true character range changes, unless they involve a change in the character where he takes a new moral action:

1. Personal success: bum-to-rich
2. Overcoming disease or addiction
3. Learning to express emotion more (having the character to cry at the end)

Again, true change of character involves the changing of the basic beliefs of the main character to take a new moral action, which is the most fundamental part of your story.

These ARE character range changes but not necessarily the best changes.

1. From animal to human or human to animal. Changing from being a mean, selfish person to a generous, compassionate person.
2. From child to adult [boy to man; girl to woman (coming of ages stories)].

3. From adult to leader; from changing the main character's way of life to changing the life of others. This is usually too preachy.
4. From recluse to participant, that is, from an isolationist to a person that participates in society.
5. From leader to tyrant. Though this is a negative change, it presents a moral argument.
6. From leader to visionary or from leader to messiah. These character types are usually those that begin as a leader of a few and progresses to expound the view of how the entire society (or at least a great portion thereof) should live. These are referred to as "Moses" stories and are many times religious stories. This can be difficult to write because you as the writer must figure out the vision of the main character and he must have a detailed moral vision. This character can also appear too preachy.

In order to construct and inject true character change into your story, first set the frame of the story; that is, start at the end of the Range of Change and then go back to the beginning and then fill the steps in between. Developing a character is a journey of learning. You as the writer must first know the character's personality and attributes along with his destination, then plot out how to get him there. The end point of his Range of Change is the character's Self-Revelation. The beginning point, of course, is the Problem/Need. The course or track that your character should take is:
Problem/Need; Desire; Opponent; Plan; Battle; ending with the character's Self-Revelation.
Start with the Self-Revelation; that is, determine what he will learn that makes his life better; then go back to his Need, his Desire and the others. Once you determine and then connect the Self-Revelation and the Need, your character is basically born. The other steps of the structure will make your character grow and mature; that is, they will develop his character. First, you must have a thinking main character that is capable of a Self-Revelation. He must also be hiding something from himself that is enslaving him and/or preventing him from having a better life. You must show the audience how he is doing this. After you determine the Self-Revelation of the main character, you must immediately determine his Need.

OBSESSIVE DRIVE

As discussed in the second step of the Classic Structure, the main character's Desire is the track that the entire story rides on and all subsequent events lead to him reaching his Goal.
In order to intensify and push the story along the Desire line track, instill within your main character an Obsessive Drive. The Obsessive Drive is a more intense form of the main character's Desire.

He is more driven to achieve his Goal. Because he now has an obsession to attain his goal, push him to take immoral steps and do almost anything to win. This will cause a decline in his character but this will show him to be human, of which the audience will almost readily relate to him. As this character drives obsessively toward his Goal, interject a "very high blocking iron wall", in the personage of the Opponent that separates and prevents him from reaching his much-desired Goal.

OPPONENT

In order to make the main character more interesting, there must be a well-developed external opposition that drives the main character. The main character is forced to grow thru the Opponent. They must drive each other to greatness.

Your story will be more interesting if you do not make your main character a totally good person and the Opponent a totally bad person. Put both of their values, originally, somewhere in the middle with both having good intentions and both having some flaws. By using these elements, you as the writer have a wide range in which to express your moral argument, which is your view of how a person should behave in the world.

The relationship between the main character and the Opponent gives your story a stronger texture. As your main character has a Goal and the Opponent has the same Goal, allow your main character to begin to lose to the opponent and force the main character to do things that he should not do in order to win. (This is discussed later in more detail.) This adds texture to the ally. Allow the ally to criticize the main character, which will force the main character to defend himself and present his moral argument. This moral argument will set up the main character's Self-Revelation, which is a key step in the structure. The Main character has something or wants the same thing that the opponent does.

These are the most powerful uses of a good Opponent:

1. Forces the main character to overcome his weakness or be destroyed.
2. Human: Have the same desire the main character to bring about direct conflict.
3. Opponent should not be the opposite of the main character. Don't have a totally good main character and totally bad opponent. Allow both to have flaws and weaknesses.

4. Keep the main character and the Opponent in same place in story. This employs the Unity of opposites, the bringing together of two different characters with different characteristics but a similar Desire.

SELF-REVELATION

This structures all of the script.
What will my main character learn at the end of the story?
How has he been wronged?
How can he live better?
He must find out how he has been wronged. Always be clear about his Self-Revelation first! Sometimes each scene is structured around frustration as a guiding principle.
The main character strips away the facade he has lived in and has a shattering moment. This shattering moment is a powerful moment where the main character has a great revelation of who he is as a person and how he should act towards others. ("Whatever doesn't kill me will make me strong.) This moment should be:

1) Sudden
2) A shattering experience that can be positive or negative
3) A burst of emotion for audience. Here the true moral need is exposed.

Distinguish between the Problem and the Need.

The Problem is the external difficultly of a situation.
The Need is something missing from within the character that must be fulfilled for a better life.

NEW EQUILIBRIUM

All is back to normal. The main character has moved to a higher or lower level. If it is a higher level, it is a positive level, which give your story more strength. Your main character has fundamentally changed. If it is a lower level, it is a negative level and your main character learns how bad he is.

The biggest problem with the steps of the Classic Structure is that there is a huge gap between the Plan and the Battle. Therefore, a fuller version of the Classic Structure is needed. The next instructs you on how to fill that huge gap.

NOTES

STRUCTURING A STRONG MIDDLE OF THE STORY

The Plan portion of the Classic Structure begins the middle of your story. In order to make and keep the middle of your story strong as you employ the steps of the classic structure, begin with the Plan of the main character, developing this step through the funnel that leads to the Battle. The first three steps of the Classic Structure have been listed and explained earlier, and here, the Plan through the Battle are detailed so that the middle of your story will keep the momentum and interest of the story that was provoked in the beginning. After an Inciting Incident moves your main character to form a Desire/Goal, he must come up with a Plan in order to fulfill his Desire/reach his Goal. Here the main character formulates strategies, schemes and tactics to help him reach his Goal. In automotive terms, the main character is the driver of the automobile; the Desire/Goal is the road and the Plan is the map that the main character uses to get to his destination. In some cases, mainly in sports, war and action stories, your hero may need and undergo some form of Training to prepare him for his Battle.

Of course, the plan must always go wrong, otherwise, the main character reaches his Goal and the story is over. Even with the abundant availability of accurate and sophisticated maps, drivers still get lost all the time for a number of reasons.

For our scriptwriting purposes, the Plan could likewise go wrong for a number of reasons of which the following are not all-inclusive:

1) The main character initially has a bad Plan.

2) The main character does not yet know how to properly implement his Plan.

3) The Opponent does something that impedes the initial Plan. By making the Plan to initially go awry, interest is added to your story because now the audience wants to see how their hero is going to readjust his Plan and/or how he is going to deal with what the Opponent does or what the Opponent has done to his original Plan. At this point, give the Opponent a plan that throws the hero's initial Plan off track. It may be good to momentarily hide the Opponent's plan that will sidetrack the hero's Plan. This will give the hero a "shock" of frustration because he thought and expected his Plan to work.

After the initial "defeat" of the hero or failure of the hero's first plan, inject in him a Drive and a will to succeed by sending him through a few series of actions of which his Plans continue to fall apart. Put him though the cycle of adjusting, then losing; re-adjusting; then losing again which will cause your hero to become desperate. This desperation will cause your main character to take immoral steps to win and will show a temporary decline of your hero. This section of your script should be the biggest section, that is, have the most number of pages.

About two-thirds through your script, you should introduce an Attack by the Ally, the conscious of the hero. Here the Ally rebukes the main character for taking immoral steps in order to reach his Goal. This brings about a controversy and dissension in trying to distinguish what the so-called "good guys" (your hero and his Allies) have done, from what the so-called "bad guys" have done. It subconsciously asks the question, "How does action reveal character?" In many stories, all of the characters are the same in that the supposed "good" characters and the "bad" characters many times do the same things (good and bad) in order to win and reach their goal. This is the continuance of the precursor to the funnel leading to the Battle. This is the one of the times that the hero and the Opponent become virtually the same in thought and action.

There is a point at which your hero feels that he has lost and it is his lowest point in the story that is his Apparent Defeat. This Apparent Defeat is not a part of the "loss" cycle of the losing and readjusting of his Plan. There is only one, clear Apparent Defeat. This must be a devastating moment for the hero. Push your hero to hit rock bottom.

This very low point leads to the main character's Obsessive Drive. Give your hero some new information that convinces him that he will reach his Goal; then intensify his Desire that pushes him to become obsessive. Bend his Desire line and force your hero to change his motive. When Dorothy was in Munchkinland, she had a Desire to go back home and a major motive was to escape the

Wicked Witch of the West. In *The Karate Kid*, Daniel initially wanted to learn karate because he had been beaten up by bullies from a karate school. He wanted to win the karate tournament that he was "forcibly" invited to attend. During the tournament, Daniel was injured and was placed on a table in the locker room. With the15-minute recovery time running out, he is "apparently defeated" and asks his mother and girlfriend to leave the room. He tells Mr. Miyagi that he wants to fight. Miyagi explains to him that there is no need for him to fight. Daniel's Desire for competing in the tournament changes from winning to completing his match so at least the guys will not think that they got the better of him and so that he could have balance with his girlfriend, Ali.

The next two sequences are short twists that continue to strengthen the middle of your story. The first is the Audience Revelation of the Opponent's ally. Give the Opponent an ally and allow the audience to know about this ally without the main character knowing who he is. This may or may not be the first time that the audience learns something that the hero does not know. This creates a superior position for the audience. You as the writer can now pull the audience back and let them see a change in your hero. The second sequence is where your hero learns all about the Opponent and his ally. Again, your hero's Desire is intensified and his will to win is even more fervent. This intensified Desire keeps the main character and the Opponent in direct conflict.

When the hero decides to take a stand; "go for broke"; "let it all hang out"; fight for (what he considers) his; in his last, best and final attempt to gain the prize (attain the Goal) he engages his Opponent in the Battle. The Battle is the clearest expression of the fight between the hero and the Opponent. The Battle takes place figuratively and many times, physically, in a narrow space and is the convergence of action, character and space. That is, the main character and Opponent are fiercely brought together in direct conflict with each other in the same place in an event that decides "who gets what". This is the crucible that tests the metal of both your hero and his Opponent. Though your hero and the Opponent are most similar at this point, you may, or should show that the hero and the Opponent are different in one or two ways. In the Battle, the theme of the story really expands for the audience because "what is at stake" is explicitly shown. The main character fulfills his Need and Desire here.

The steps of the Classic Structure from the Plan through the Battle comprises the middle of your script all the way to the "beginning of the ending." The ending contains the Self-Revelation and the New Equilibrium, both of which were explained earlier.

NOTES

DIALOGUE

The story is carried in the dialogue. However, dialogue does not carry the story. Structure carries the story.

Dialogue is the quickest window into the mind of the character. Dialogue should always move the story forward and reveal something about the character's attitudes, perceptions and it also expresses the values of the character. These are the stated beliefs and values of the character; the cares, likes and dislikes of the character. These values are also the character's view of what is valuable in life. At times, the character may explore these values through questioning. For example, one character may ask another whether or not he should tell his wife of his past extramarital affair or not tell her and return to being good and faithful to her.

Dialogue is the order of the main character's development thru the various scenes. Good dialogue must sound like real talk and be real talk; it must sound natural.

Always write for the reader of the script.

Emphasize strong active verbs.

Develop a unique style.

Do not put in camera angles or a lot of directorial direction and information.

These guidelines will help you to develop good dialogue.

DIRECT & INDIRECT PLAN

Here, the desire of the characters drive the scene and divulges what plan that character will use to achieve this goal.

Direct plan dialogue is when the character says directly what he wants.

Indirect plan dialogue is when the character says that he wants one thing while really wanting something else. The other character will:

1) Recognize this and go along with it.
or
2) Not recognize the deception and be fooled.

OPPOSING VALUES

One character states his beliefs; the second character gives an opposing view. Then there is an attack and defense of each other's position.

MORAL ARGUMENT

Character one supports a course of action. Character two says that course of action is wrong. Character one defends himself; then there is an attack and defense about that course of action.

There are two terms that are very closely related in definition and usage and their usage is more a matter of who is using the terms that determines when they are applied.
These terms are Foreshadowing and Exposition.

FORESHADOWING

This is hinting about an event that will take place later. It is mostly a suggestion or indication of something that is coming up. Foreshadowing sets up the story situation for something that will come in the near or distant future. Don't provide too much advance information on an upcoming event because:

1) The upcoming event is still in the future and this event has not yet been seen.
2) Too much information is difficult to absorb.

EXPOSITION

Exposition is important background information given to the audience that assists in the understanding of the story. To be effective, Exposition must be exposed in a way that this needed information is revealed in a natural and interesting way that *does not stop or slow down the story.*

Exposition communicates the necessary facts of the story. Do not give the audience any more information than is necessary to understand the story. Do not reveal too much too soon. Let your characters keep their secrets as long as they can. Saving up Exposition and using it in crucial moments will make it more exciting and even transform it into a turning point. Do not allow one character to tell the other something he/she already knows: "We've been married ten years now, honey". Some Exposition can be handled without dialogue. It is always better to show than tell. Since movies are a visual medium, showing the character and revealing the character's traits visually is much better than talking heads telling about the character.

Avoid these in Exposition dialogue:

1. Do not slow down or stop the story.
2. Do not reveal a lot of information about a character, place or situation that has not yet been seen.

   It is hard to remember a lot of information about a character that has not yet been introduced and it is probably even harder to care about that character. One or two pre-meeting facts are usually okay but not a whole history and list of facts about a character, place or situation that has not yet been introduced.
3. "As you know" dialogue is very awkward dialogue. People usually don't hold conversations about information that they both already know. If they do, it is usually very boring conversation and it will make very boring dialogue in a script.
4. "Out of left field" dialogue is where a character spurts out some information that jumps out from nowhere, from out of the blue. That is, the character spurts out information that is not consistent with the ongoing conversation. In reality it usually causes one person to either express verbally or in a facial expression, "Where did that come from?" In reality this is awkward and it is equally awkward in a script.

5. Avoid long **flashbacks** and dream sequences. Seldom do flashbacks move the story forward. Use flashbacks ONLY if they move the story FORWARD. Do not give Exposition in a flashback unless it motivates the story and/or moves it forward.

Use Exposition through conflict; conflict between characters. Express exposition through the desire line; that is, express what the person wants or wants to achieve. Always be aware of the range of change. Good drama is conflict between two characters and what they believe in: the beliefs of the main character vs. those of the Opponent. Exposition can be made exciting by having characters argue over it. Every dialogue scene should involve some conflict.

A great university scriptwriting instructor, Professor Charles Deemer, has this to say about dialogue:

DON'T LET WRITING GET IN THE WAY OF YOUR STORY

Term after term, year after year, I keep seeing the same errors, especially early on before students begin to understand how different screenwriting is from all other narrative forms. Here then is my list of the most common errors, in no particular order.

Fiction Rhetoric. Many of my students come from a fiction background, and it immediately shows. They overwrite at every level. They describe too much. Their sentence structure is too complex. Their paragraphs are too long, giving the script great text density and the look of a literary document. Here are some guidelines to avoid fiction rhetoric:

- Write in simple sentences only. Remember what a complex sentence is? It is a sentence with a subordinate clause. Avoid them like the plague! They slow down a quick reading and all screenplays are read quickly, even skimmed, before they are read carefully. Direct, simple sentences. Don't be afraid to use sentence fragments. Pretend you're in Junior High.
- Write in short paragraphs. Each paragraph should take no more than four or five lines across the page before you double space and start a new one. This opens up the script, making it vertical, making it easier to read. If there is a new subject, a new focus, start a new paragraph. Though you can't "direct the film" in a spec script, you can in a way by your paragraph spacing. Make each paragraph a new shot.

- Too much description. You are not the costume designer. Every time you describe a piece of clothing or something in a room, anything, ask yourself: is this *essential* or is it an option? Is Mary's red coat necessary? If the coat is blue, does her character change or the story fall apart? Get rid of the options, letting your collaborators make the decisions, and retain the essentials.

Expository dialogue. In general, dialogue is a clumsy way to communicate facts and figures. It takes skill to pull it off. Until you reach this level of craft, avoid doing it. Find other ways to relate essential information, preferably visually.

Chit chat. The problem with most dialogue in beginners' screenplays, is that too much of it goes nowhere. It is realistic, yes, but life moves much more slowly than a well crafted story does. Again, the final test is elimination: if you remove this line of dialogue, what happens? Do the screenplay and story collapse into incomprehensible gibberish? Is an essential character trait lost? If nothing happens, then why is it there? Like descriptive writing, keep your dialogue lean and mean. Exchanges of dialogue that are short and quick play much better, in general, than wordy exchanges.

NOTES

GENRE

By definition, genre is: categorizing by kind, sort or type. Genre refers to the story elements such as romance in a love story, humor in a comedy, the horror element in a horror story, etc. Each Genre has its own thematic argument its own particular type of hero. Each Genre takes place on a particular social stage. Genre and Structure are not the same thing. As discussed earlier, Structure is the arrangement of scenes that reveals character and unfolds action; it is the framework and path of the story. Don't allow your story Genre to interfere with your ability to build a powerful Structure for your script. Genre supports Structure but it does not replace Structure. It is common for writers to believe that a romantic comedy must unfold in a certain way; and an action movie must unfold another way. These are damaging limits to the use of Genre. Great Story Structure transcends the potentially stifling traditional Genre definitions and elements that attempt to limit and stifle it.

Genre will never be a successful substitute for story structure. Perhaps people choose to see a particular movie because of its genre; but it is the story structure that holds the story together and it is structure that moves the story through the elements of that particular genre.

The best way to use genre is to bend, mix and transcend it. That is, instead of writing according to the rigid definition of a particular Genre, bend it or be more flexible in your writing within a drama. For instance, if you are writing a love story, do not always adhere to the love story genre. You may, and probably should, mix your love story with some action. Also, if you are writing an action story, transcend it and mix it by employing the elements of the detective, horror and gangster genre.

Definitions and examples

The definitions and examples of Genre used here are sub-structures of the Classic Structure and will differ from the classic Hollywood definitions. This creates more mutually understandable terms and concepts. For example, a Western does not necessarily take place in the 1870's, etc. It takes place at the turning point of barbarianism and civilization. Defining and using Genre by these means will allow you to expand your story and make it more unique.

If you look up any movie's Genre, most times you will discover that there are two or more listed Genres. For instance, if you look up Backdraft you may find that it is listed as an Action/Drama/Mystery/Thriller. Hence, the use of two or more other Genres blended together. This is a classic example of Mixing a Genre which will expand and strengthen your story and make it more interesting. Below are listed at least 5 ways to use Genre in the expanding and strengthening of your story and making it more interesting.

1) Repeat the Genre: Take old, used story and write it again. Even though each Genre has its own philosophy, to repeat a Genre is to re-write a known story-type, only with different characters. The problem with repeating a Genre is that there is no new thinking or surprise.

2) Undercut the Genre: Tell the Genre story in the same Classic Structure but reverse the audience's expectations; that is, do the opposite of what that particular Genre calls for.
For example, write an anti-western or anti-detective story by starting out in the traditional sense of the Genre, then do the opposite of and go against the traditional way that that particular Genre unfolds. Though this is a unique and powerful way to use Genre, the primary problem is that your story may lack reality.

3) Transcend the Genre: Go beyond the usual elements and definitions of the Genre. Take a kind-helper, angel-type character and put him in the center of an Action story. This character usually comes in and solves other people's problems and leaves. You transcend this Genre by giving this character problems and needs of his own. When you transcend a Genre, make a personal statement and give your personal vision of how a character should act/react within the story instead of allowing the Genre to dictate what the character should do. In the traditional love story, boy meets girl; boy likes girl; boy pursues girl; boy gets girl; and many times, boy loses girl. Transcend the Genre by: boy meets girl; boy likes girl but will not play girl's game of cat and mouse; boy ignores girl; girl

pursues boy; girl gets boy; girl likes boy's friend; boy likes girl's friend; neither know how to tell the other.

4) Bend the Genre: Though you stay within the Genre, make it more flexible by allowing the traditional aspects of that Genre to go somewhat "off of the beaten path". In an Action story, some of the bad guys may be convicted but the main villain beats the rap. In a Detective story, all of the clues of the brilliant detective may lead to the right place but the wrong person is temporarily apprehended while the real perpetrator works within the police department. This creates a more engaging story.

5) Mix the Genre: Blend two or more Genres into one story. The element of surprise is likely and it creates a richer story.

There are some Genres that are **difficult** (not impossible) to mix:

A. Love Story with Horror
B. Action with Fairy Tale
C. Gangster with Fairy Tale

Included below are the major Genres with different definitions (as previously mentioned) and applications from the traditional Hollywood definitions.

DRAMA

Drama is a sequence of events where someone is acting upon someone else. In this discourse, there usually is a moral choice that leads to a change of actions. Because Drama is an integral component and is a necessary, cohesive ingredient in almost all stories, it deserves to be elevated to a super genre or distinguished category. A story of a particular Genre can be easily written with the exclusion of any other Genre and still be a good, interesting story. However, it is difficult, almost impossible, to write almost any story Genre without at least some aspect of Drama.

The characteristics of this category are:

1) The main character has a strong Ghost.

2) The Desire comes relatively early, though not as early as in a Fairy Tale. And unlike the Fairy Tale, achieving the Goal is more difficult.
3) This is usually set in the pressure cooker of a single arena.
4) There is an intimate opponent, usually within the family of the main character.
5) The revelations that the main character receives are almost always a Self-Revelation.

Though these are not negatives, the weaknesses of the Drama category are:

1) It gives a portion or slice of life in great detail but it does not give the big picture.
2) Usually does not expand to the universal level. It's story in regional. That is, the story is not expansive to the point of widespread inclusiveness. Its story is in the realm of the intimate world of the hero and Opponent.
3) It is too realistic.

All of the above "weaknesses" of Drama can be manipulated to create a powerful story. These "weaknesses" are not to be avoided; rather they are to be utilized and blended within the various Genres to strengthen that particular Genre.

The strengths of a Drama are:

1) It has complex and real characters.
2) The hero and the Opponent both have weaknesses and strengths.
3) It emphasizes choice as opposed to destiny.
4) The opposition is an intimate opposition to the point that the more intimate the opposition, the more powerful the story.

HORROR

This genre involves something inhuman trying to become human by entering the human realm. The Opponent wants to belong to the human community. It asks the most fundamental question of what is human and what is inhuman. Horror involves the "haunted house" whereas the hero is trapped and cannot leave a particular place. The characters are reduced mostly metaphorically to animals and machines. The "animal" aspect of the character involves a fear of losing control of himself. The "machine" character fears a loss of personal identity.

Two steps are emphasized in the Horror Genre:

1. An external (monster)
2. An internal (ghost) attack.

The monster is the personification of what we fear most, and then it attacks. The ghost is the power of the past on the present. This is exemplified by the effects of the sins of a father or mother on their children of which these patterns cannot be broken. Ghost is made physical by forcing your hero to live in a "haunted house". The haunted house is almost always an enclosed place/space (not necessarily a house) where the hero cannot escape.

A good way to undercut this Genre is to flip between human and inhuman characters and the "monster" becomes the hero in the middle of the story. Make the inhuman character to actually be human and the human to be an animal. E.T. at first is the "monster" then he is realized as being good. The human adults and scientists turn out to be monsters; they want to dissect and study E.T. In The Shining, the Ghost is the fact that the former caretaker killed his family.

To transcend this Genre:

1) The hero should become a monster but remain human.
2) The hero's monstrosity occurs against his own family or someone close to him.
3) Reduce the hero to brutality.

Here are a few popular movies from the Horror Genre.

MISERY: The Kathy Bates character (Annie) is monstrous and human in her treatment of the James Caan character (Paul Sheldon). Paul is also injured, incapacitated and trapped within Annie's house, thus, there is a "haunted house".

THE EXORCIST: A young girl, Regan, is possessed by a monster that is attempting to exist in the human realm. In this case, Regan's bedroom becomes the "haunted house" for the exorcising priests.

JURRASIC PARK: The island becomes a "haunted house" because those that are attempting to escape are trapped on the island.

ALIENS: The crew of the spacecraft is trapped in their spacecraft in outer space with a monster.

JAWS: Three men are trapped in the ocean on a small boat, which is being attacked by a huge shark. The boat is a "haunted house" in that they cannot safely leave the boat while in the ocean.

FRANKENSTEIN: Initially, the monster is beaten, burned and whipped; then he is shown to be human with a little girl. When the little girl drowns, he is hunted by the townspeople that turn into monsters in their pursuit of him.

WESTERN

This is the story of the bully; lawlessness and the attempted containment of lawlessness. This is the Good guy going after the Bad guy. It asks the question, "Who is the baddest of us all?" The Battle is the most emphasized step of the Structure.

Examples:
THE UNTOUCHABLES: This is a mixture of the Gangster in a Western Action story whereas Eliot Ness decides to fight against Al Capone.

JAMES BOND FILMS: James Bond matches wits against his foe in a "Last man standing" duel.

BATMAN: Batman attempts to contain the lawlessness of his Opponents.

BRAVEHEART: William Wallace rallies his countrymen in an attempt to contain the lawlessness of Longshanks and there are Battles to determine who will rule Scotland.

STAR WARS: Luke Skywalker, along with his allies, battle to contain the attempted expansion and rule of the Empire.

ACTION

This is the outgrowth of the classic western: masculine versus feminine approach; fight or flight. It is the "Man Who Fights" of which the Battle is emphasized over all of the other steps in the Classic Structure. The main character's strength is his ability to take action and the proper approach for the main character in the Action story is to always stand and fight. The hero usually has a good plan and training and he usually well executes his Plan. There is an emphasis on the hero's improvisation and his changing in a moment.

This Genre is very popular because:

1. The Desire line is very clear and the track of the story can run at a high speed.
2. It has a propensity to emphasize the pace and speed of the story over the content. It does not require a lot of detailed development.
3. The main character and the Opponent are simplistic in a very fast paced story.

To transcend the Action Genre:

1) Give your hero a sense of humor so that his humor undercuts his pretentiousness.
2) Place your story in a single arena, which will cause a "pressure cooker effect" that explodes in the final Battle.
3) Make the opponent human and give him defendable views.
4) Start with a low Desire line and a simple Goal.
5) Add texture to the story by placing your hero on one edge of the stage where he has to adapt or be destroyed.

GANGSTER

This is the story of Rank, Privilege, Power and Hierarchy. It is not always the traditional street gangster of a city but most times it is. This Genre asks the questions: "What is the difference between true success and false success" and "What constitutes success?" To get ahead, one must fight. The story is the corruption of the American Dream. It is a king in a democracy. This story is classified as the "Man who kills", distinguishing itself from the Action story classification of the "Man who fights". This Genre has a unique story line, which is a rise and fall.

Structuring the Gangster Genre places immoral, dastardly and menacing emphasis on:

1. Desire: The Goal is always an illegal Goal.
2. Plan: The method to carry out his plan involves the use of some type of weaponry.
3. Opponent: The Opponent is sometimes an officer of the law.

These are examples of the Gangster Genre.
SCARFACE: This is the tagline from the Internet Movie Database for the Al Pacino starrer, "In the spring of 1980 the port at Mariel Harbor was opened, and thousands set sail for the United States. They came in search of the American Dream. One of them found it on the sun washed avenues of Miami…wealth, power and passion beyond his wildest dreams. He was Tony Montana but the world will remember him by another name…Scarface". This tagline is very similar to our description of the classic Gangster story. Note the terms "American Dream", "wealth and power".

THE GODFATHER: Don Corleone is a likable hero in this story because, though he is the head of a mafioso family, he is very humanistic in his character.

CALIGULA: This movie is included to serve as an example of biopics about despots. Films about Hitler, Stalin, Idi Amin and other cruel dictators (probably a redundancy) are examples of Gangsters. The differences from the traditional street gangster is that they are not in search of the "American Dream", but they are very much concerned with Rank, Privilege, Power and Hierarchy. They are also very much epitomized by the "Man who kills" classification.

DETECTIVE

The Detective story asks "who is good/bad; guilty/innocent: who did it"? The Detective is usually a person who searches for truth, reason and meaning. Many times his superior emerges as an annoying, secondary opponent.

The Detective usually has two positive attributes:

1. He has a good, powerful mind and capacity for problem solving.
2. He can get the job done.

The primary weakness of this Genre is that the Opponent (the one sought by the Detective) is hidden. You can strengthen this Genre by creatively using any of the previously listed ways to use Genre.

Here are some ways to Transcend this Genre:

1. Give the Detective his own Problem and Need. This will create a track of the Detective's personal life.
2. Set up a one-to-connection between the problem that the Detective is attempting to solve and his personal problem(s).
3. Make the Detective partly responsible for what went wrong in his investigation and make him learn of his complicity in what went wrong.
4. When the Detective learns of his personal responsibility, give him a revelation which will cause him to take a new moral action.
5. Show the Detective's acts of searching for truth as being destructive and beneficial.

Examples:
BEVERLY HILLS COP: Axel Foley traveled from Detroit to Beverly Hills in search of murderers.

SAVING PRIVATE RYAN: Of course this is a war movie but it has many of the elements of the Detective story. Though there was no search for guilt or innocence, good or bad, the men under Captain's Miller command in searching for Private Ryan did falsely assume that Private Ryan was a bad guy. Upon finding and meeting him, they had a revelation.

BACKDRAFT: This movie genre is listed as: Action/Drama/Mystery/Thriller. Though it certainly has some aspects of all of those, it is primarily a Detective story in that the fire fighters were on a tenacious search to find the arsonist.

GHOST: Though the sentimental aspect of this story involves the intense love of Sam and Molly, most of the story involves Sam doing Detective work.

THE LOVE STORY

This is the most likely Genre where one person grows thru another person. The main character has a unique need, which can only be fulfilled by one other person. The lover must always be necessary to the main character and vice versa. It asks, "What do lovers give to each other that makes each individual a complete person?" The main character must learn to balance his individual desires and sacrifices for someone else.

He loves in spite of his lover's:

1. Opposition
2. Imperfection
3. Differences from him

A great love story is about trust and forgiveness.

There are 2 points in the Classic Structure that are emphasized.

1. Desire
2. Opposition: Usually the opponent is the lover.

Standing alone, this is a peculiar Genre because:

1. There is no real, defined hero and there is little action.
2. There are two equally well-defined characters, though one is more dominant.
3. Many times, the deepest opponent is love itself.

To write a great, strong Love Story, mix your Genres. In the purest form of the Love Story, there is very little story in that two people meet or already know each other, they fall in love and go off to live happily ever after. To create a more complete, interesting story you must create the Action (opposition) each one takes against the other person. Be aware of creating characters that are either different enough to sustain opposition (among themselves) once they fall in love or create outside opposition to them. Otherwise, the story is over once they fall in love. Also, give your characters an intense, unique Need. They must have strong needs based on strong weaknesses. Give your characters very strong passion to the point that they are "crazy" about each other. Each character must grow because of the other.

The key to the Love Story is that the main characters must be seen together. The audience must feel that the two characters must be together.

Examples
ROCKY: Rocky's Need of self esteem, companionship and love qualifies and defines this movie as a Love Story. Even at the end of a heavyweight championship fight in which he may be the potential winner of a split decision, Rocky ignores the announcer's reading of the judge's scorecards. His only focus is on, "Adrian"!!!

TITANIC: The fate of the ship and the lives of a couple thousand people are secondary to the love affair between Jack and Rose.

COMEDY

This shows the dramatic, slow decline and rise of a character or characters and these characters being dropped and set-up many times during the course of the story.
The hero is reduced to an animal, child, machine or a mixture of these. (Lucy; Pee-Wee Herman; Adam Sandler to name a few.) The reduction of the character to these attributes is not necessarily a negative or bad action, it is simply the process of comedic situations.

Animal: Characters engage in some form of repulsive behavior.
"Dirty" jokes; bathroom humor; basic body functions; actions that would ordinarily be very dangerous and/or harmful. (The Three Stooges)

Child: characters literally act as a child or over-reacts to a situation.

Machine: characters literally act like an object or a machine with obviously understated dead pan emotion.

The challenge of writing Comedy is that you must create humor, something that is funny to someone else and you must devise a structure that produces gags and humor. It is difficult or next to impossible to create a formula and teach someone how to write something that will be funny to someone else. Even the most popular comedians test their work through stand-up before a "test" audience, they report that many times their material is bad, not funny and falls flat to their audience.

Here are some suggestions, nonetheless, that will aid you in creating your Comedy.

1. Give your main character a low Goal but make him exert intense efforts to reach an ordinarily easy Goal.
2. Though your main character exerts his best efforts, he has pitiful, somewhat loathsome abilities.
3. Move your main character toward a chaotic Battle where everyone is incompetent.

The definition, classification and descriptions of the Comedy Genre are plain, precise and unambiguous. Therefore, no examples of the Comedy Genre are listed.

MYTHS/FAIRY TALES & FANTASY

MYTHS

These are fictitious stories that involve a phenomenon of nature. They also involve the character's supernatural exploits. (The Matrix; Superman; The Wizard of Oz)

FAIRY TALES

These are fictitious stories that involve the ideal, virtually enviable, legendary exploits of humans.

The key aspects of Fairy Tales are:

1) The Problem, Need and Desire come almost immediately.

2) It is often a story literally about slavery; caught in a castle; a dungeon; a system; anything in which the character feels trapped.
3) The characters are divided into extremes of good and evil.
4) There is an extreme Desire line.
5) The story is almost always becoming successful.

The primary weakness of this Genre for you to overcome is that the solution to the struggle of the main character is many times a passive, longsuffering solution. Therefore, you should move the main character to create his solution to his problem. Sleeping Beauty sleeps for 100 years before being kissed by the Prince. This is a passive moment in that she is acted on by the Prince as opposed to committing an act herself that is the resolution to her problem.

Good examples of the main character being active in creating his own solution:
(Pretty Woman; Working Girl; The Secret of my Success)

FANTASY

These are stories that intentionally depart from reality and are supernatural in its creation.
(Toy Story; Shark Tale; Finding Nemo; Peter Pan)

All three of these story types are usually:

1. Highly imaginative
2. Unrestricted by reality
3. Set on an unreal or surreal social stage

MONSTERS & DEMONS

These are afflictions (sickness; physical/mental malady) of the main character; natural disasters (tornado; hurricane; earthquake; fire, etc) that acts upon the main character.
(*Stepmom*; *Dying Young*; *Twister*; *Towering Inferno*; *Poseidon Adventure*; *The Perfect Storm* (part Horror: Haunted House).

The Genre is unique in that there is no direct human Opponent to the main character. The Opponent is the monster or demon. The subplot involves creating a community of opposites, which are allies and opponents that offer views and values that are for or against the hero and others within the group. This group creates the sounding board of the audience. The human opponent is present in the community.

There must be a strong opponent within the group in order to:

1. Intensify the hardship for the main character.
2. Create the stage for the friendly and opposing views of the community, which is the line of connection to the audience.

MIXED GENRE

Here is a short list of examples of Mixed Genre.

STAR WARS (Horror/Western)
ROCKY (Action/Love Story)
AN OFFICER AND A GENTLEMAN (Love Story/Action/Adventure)
TITANIC (Horror/Love Story)
ONE FLEW OVER THE CUCKOO'S NEST (Horror/Comedy)
WITNESS (Horror/Detective/Love)
JURASSIC PARK (Western/Horror)

NOTES

MAKING YOUR WRITING VISUAL

SOCIAL STAGE

In writing your story, you must master two different forms of communication; one is story (words) and the other is visual. The world that your main character lives in must join with the world of your story; therefore, you must create and develop a visual world. This world is an expression of and helps to delineate who the main character is.

Along with applying the Classic Structure, the story should take place in a specific community/ Social Stage. Location is very important. After the setting that is appropriate for the main character is determined, establish and describe the setting of the story.

You must create a "world"/society for the main character. This world is an expression of the main character and will help define him. This world and community is directly linked to the hero and either assists or hinders the actions of him. The Social Stage is the soil and community of the main character. To create this world, you must determine the Arena of the hero. The arena is a single, unified place, inhabited by the main character that is expandable.
Example: the house; the bar; the small town; the city; the flat plain; the ocean; outer space.
Keep main character in a single arena. The misconception is that the Main Character should go everywhere.

CREATING THE SINGLE ARENA

1. The Shrinking Universe: At first the audience is shown the big picture, then this can be condensed; cross-cut within the arena.

Ex. Aliens in outer space to a planet to a particular place on the planet to a haunted house.
2. The Linear Journey: The main character takes a single line journey and moves toward his Goal. All of the territory that is passed thru is generally the same. In "road pictures", the opponent must be brought along with the main character.
3. The Circular Journey: The main character moves in a certain direction. He has movement, but it is usually in one space.

FISH OUT OF WATER

This is a Social Stage where someone is out of his or her normal environment or range of activities. There are two arenas here that start in one Arena but little time is spent there. Establish the main character's talents that are unique to this environment, then go to the second (main) arena. The main character in the first environment is contrasted to the second environment, but will adapt the same talents of the first world to the second world.
Examples:
Beverly Hills Cop: Axel Foley is from the streets of Detroit. His street smarts are very useful in Beverly Hills.
Crocodile Dundee: A man from the Australian Outback is taken to New York City whereas his outback roots help him to survive in the jungle of the city.
Rush Hour: A Chinese police officer goes to Los Angeles on a kidnapping investigation and employs the same detective acumen in L.A. that he used in China.

There are 5 stages of the Social Stage and each one has a unique Main character.

1) Social Stage: the wilderness/village; main character: superhero (prevalent in classical Westerns)
2) Social Stage: city; main character: the fragile hero (everyone here is on the edge)
3) Social Stage: the oppressive city; main character: the anti-hero
4) Social Stage: the anti-community; main character: the visionary hero
5) Social Stage: the town/house; main character: "everyman" in that every type of character originates and inhabits this space.

Wilderness/Village: emphasizes potential for growth
The Village is chosen because of its perceived lack of sophistication. The superhero must emerge. The Wilderness/Village is a fragile society that has just begun to set roots and expand. It is surrounded by the City that wants to impose its will upon the Wilderness/Village. From this scenario, the classic hero emerges who is capable of defeating the invaders, and he does. The values in the Wilderness/Village are martial in that force must be used to solve their problems that involve the invaders. This world has some degree of tolerance, cooperation and decency. The main character determines that the distinction between good and evil are very strong here. The Wilderness/Village is prevalent in the Western; the city cop also emerges from the village. Example: Dirty Harry

The City is a place of levels of the rich and powerful in high places. The middle class is psychologically, metaphorically and physically on the outskirts of the City and the poor are on the streets. The City is analogous to the jungle in detective stories. This is the world where there is technology and levels of power bureaucracy. Its characters live in a "dog eat dog" world where everyone lives on the edge of a major life occurrence. Their movement is at an accelerated pace within and outside of the City. It is a place of opportunity and failure and many times has an average main character who is concerned with justice and stopping the enslavement of bureaucracy. In this stage, the main characters are usually females or they at least are integral parts of the story. *In One Flew Over the Cuckoo's Nest*, McMurphy goes against the rigid rules of Nurse Ratched and he attempts to "free" his allies from his perceived bureaucratic enslavement.

An expansion of the City, the Oppressive City, is a big, technological city that was supposed to improve but now oppresses and enslaves. The Oppressive City is a society of people on the move. This society is aggressively idealistic and attempts to spread their idealism, usually into the anti-Community. The main character (an anti-hero) will not conform and he is either sent out or coerced into conformity. An example of this character type is Luke in *Cool Hand Luke* though he is in the anti-Community.

The anti-Community prides itself on being a virtually segregated society where conformity is the rule and outsiders are not welcome. This society psychologically enslaves the inhabitants into its particular culture. Going against the grain, the main character emerges in an attempt to enlighten the society. To make and keep this Social Stage interesting, the main character's views are of utmost importance in this society. Therefore, he must either remain in this arena or if he leaves, he must return. The main character should spend a great deal of time in this arena in order to make this Social Stage of any valuable interest to the audience.

The Town/House has sense of community; kids playing; neighbors talking. It creates a sense of harmony and coordination.

A House is a paradoxical unity of opposites. It could be a place of happiness that contains a family or it could be a place of slavery as in the "haunted house". In many instances, Ghost was born within the House.

Use your creativity with locations within the house to reveal the soul of a character. For instance, you can use a cellar to depict a vast array of adverse situations or reveal various dastardly acts, past or present. These scenarios traditionally follow the Horror Genre. Using a cellar is not strictly a Horror Genre location, but it is primarily a symbol of negativity and bad occurrences. Evil can occur anywhere but there are some places that are not exactly bastions of good.

An attic is also a powerful location but it can be more flexible. The positive aspects of an attic can be used by making it the place where a character's cherished items are stored; such as diaries, photographs and other memorabilia. However, like the cellar, it can also be a place of evil and/or bad memories. The same place that houses cherished items can also house some very painful, loathsome items.

Passageways can be used in the same ways as cellars and attics. Narrow passageways normally metaphorically depict some aspect of the will to escape to another place. Broad passageways depict spaciousness and freedom.

In *The Wizard of Oz*, Dorothy's attitude and actions were different in Kansas than they were in Munchkin Land and in Oz. She also behaved differently in the pleasantries of Munchkinland and Oz than she did in the witch's castle.
In *An Officer and a Gentleman*, Zack Mayo behaved differently on base (in training) than he did as a boy in the Philippines. The base was a safer surrounding than the streets of the Philippines.

NOTES

INVALUABLE INFORMATION NOT RELATED TO STRUCTURE

Make your screenplay vertical. It is much easier to read a script, or any manuscript for that matter, that has a lot of white space on the page than one that has great text density. This is because the eye can race down a page in a kind of vertical reading style much easier than dragging across a page horizontally. For quick reading, for skimming, the page that invites vertical eye movement is much friendlier to a hurried reader. Unless you are a person that has sold top box office generating scripts, the person that will be reading your script will definitely be a hurried reader. Make sure that your screenplay can be scanned and skimmed very easily. Open up your writing by using short paragraphs (about five lines or less) and simple sentences. Stay away from complex sentences and wordy rhetoric.

THE MYTH OF THE THREE ACT STRUCTURE

Scriptwriting professor Charles Deemer says emphatically, "I believe that the three act structure is overrated" and "Don't worry about three distinct acts. You may find that a five act structure works better for your screenplay. It worked for Shakespeare. You may have a good story that just naturally breaks down into four acts. Squeezing it into the Procrustean bed of Three Act Structure is just going to mangle it."

Professor Deemer further states, "A lot has been written in screenwriting books about Three-Act Structure. The basic idea of drama having three acts goes back to Aristotle. Here is an example of how it works: In the beginning, or first act, you get your hero up a tree. In the middle, or second act, he tries to get out of the tree, but ends up even further up the tree. In the finale, or last act, he climbs down or falls out of the tree."

That much is true, but it's not saying much. It's pretty difficult to write a story without a beginning, middle and end.

Those terms, however, are just useful shorthand. "First act" is simply a convenient way to talk about the beginning of the story without someone having to ask, "Do you mean the beginning shot, the beginning scene, the first reel, the first half, what?"

Here is the model of the three act breakdown,

First Act: the beginning
Second Act: the middle
Third Act: the end

Most screenwriting instructors teach that your first act should be 25 to 35 pages long and that your second act should end around page 90. At the end of each act is a "turning point" where the hero's situation drastically changes, his desires change, and the flow of the story turns. They further teach that there is also a "flex point" around page 60 where the situation intensifies.

This may be the case in a lot of stories. A lot of high-concept off-the-rack thrillers do have hard "act" breaks. It is also true that in the majority of movies, the story is going full force by no later than the first quarter; things get complicated in the middle half; and everything comes together for a climax in the last quarter.

However, only perhaps half of all great movies have three distinct acts, and in some of those, you have to stretch to figure out where exactly the act breaks are. For instance, where are the act breaks in *Spartacus*? *Forrest Gump*; *The Wizard of Oz*; *The Fugitive*; *Apollo 13*; or the superbly written *Wild Things*, which has about five or six major "twists"?

One could no doubt dissect these films and come up with their idea of where the act breaks are, but how important is it to know where the act breaks are and how will that help you write a good script?

Even if you could determine where the act breaks are in a long list of films, how would that help you to understand how to write a good story and, for our particular purposes, structure a good script?

A story can fail in its beginning, its middle or its end, but knowing where you are in the script will not necessarily help you fix the story.

The important thing is to tell a story that will be interesting to your audience. A story can certainly fail structurally. Also, just because you know how to structure a script doesn't mean that your script will necessarily be good. There are a lot of athletes that know how to play baseball, hockey, basketball, football or whatever sport; it doesn't mean that they can play well.

If an athlete is not as proficient in a sport as they like to be, they should do the same thing that a scriptwriter does if a script is not good. They should continue to study and practice their craft.

In the big picture, however, if you have a script that a producer or someone with "juice" wants to see, by all means know where the act breaks are and be prepared to tell them in detail about the three acts.

Though it is good for you to learn how to break your story down into the "three act structure," learn and apply the Classic Structure to script, which will make it rock solid.

ALSO FROM PROFESSOR DEEMER:

COMMON SCRIPTWRITING MISTAKES

When you teach screenwriting as I do, and read over 100 student scripts a year, it doesn't take long before you get a sense of the kinds of mistakes most student screenwriters make in the beginning. Here is my summary of the most important of them.

Lack of Story Clarity

It's astounding how many of my students cannot give a brief, focused answer to the question, "What is your story about?" Usually the question elicits rambling monologues that go on forever. By the end of them, I know less about the story than when I asked the question.

Story clarity is essential in a screenplay. If the story has no focus, no story spine, on which to hang all the episodes and actions along the way, then it's far too easy for the reader/audience to get lost, far too easy to see the energy of the story dissipate rather than beam into one, intense direction for a singular effect.

A good way to test your story clarity is with a logline. There really are two uses of loglines: for pitching the story *after* it is written, which is the common use. But I also use loglines in my classes as a writer's tool. A logline can be a guide and reminder of the central focus of the story. "An estranged husband cross-dresses as a nanny in order to visit his children." That's a good logline. "A lonely boy befriends a stranded alien and rescues him from government capture so he can return home." There's another. Can you write as succinct a logline for your own story? If you have story clarity, you should be able to.

"May I get you a drink?": The Waiter Syndrome, or Poor Scene Design

Scene design is about when scenes begin and when scenes end. Beginning writers, and a lot of pro's in their early drafts, begin scenes too soon and end scenes too late.

Let's look at an example. I use *The Birdcage* in class because Elaine May's script has excellent scene design. There's a moment when Armand and his son are wondering how to pass themselves off as a normal family for the visit of the conservative future in-laws. Armand gets the idea of drafting the boy's real mother, long out of the picture, to pose as the mother of the family. That's the action. It's presented this way: Armand makes the suggestion and the son replies, "Wow, do you think she'd really do it?" The cut is to the mother *already on the phone*, saying, Armand! It's been years!

A beginning writer not only would continue the conversation between father and son: "Of course she would; Really? Why not?" etc., but would prolong the scene to show Armand finding a phone booth, looking up a number, dialing, the mother's secretary answers, and so on. May's cut is from the meat of the scene to the middle of the response.

Study movies for their scene transitions. You can learn a lot about good, efficient design.

Chat, chat, chat, ho-hum: Pointless dialogue

Many of my screenwriting students would be better off in a playwriting class. They write long, talky scenes more suited to the stage, where dialogue is the primary tool for story exposition and movement. In film, however, dialogue is *not* the primary tool, visual storytelling is.

I recently showed *E.T.* to my University screenwriting class. Look at that movie again and notice how much of the story is told without dialogue. In fact, no important dramatic moments in that movie are dialogue scenes. Dialogue is a kind of filler between the visual scenes, giving us details of story and character that we need to expand the more essential strokes of the images.

There's an easy way to test dialogue in a script. Cut it and see what is lost. If nothing is lost, leave it out!

Remember, dialogue in a screenplay must move the story forward or reveal character, and preferably both at the same time. Take out the chain saw and rid your script of all idle chit chat.

Director wannabes

Director wannabes are always writing about what the camera is doing. We see this and we see that. In the contemporary screenplay, the writer does not direct the camera in any way. If you are telling the audience a particular way it sees a scene, then you are being a director. Don't be.

So how do you tell a story visually without directing the camera? Easily. You include the images important to the story but not the particular angles at which these images are seen.

There are several ways to isolate important images in your storytelling. One is to isolate them in separate paragraphs, which also opens up your script to include a lot of white space. And just your choice of detail suggests images that are important. For example, in the script to *E.T.* early on, mention is made that the arriving humans are anonymous and that one is known by his dangling keys. On film, this translated to shots of legs and feet, and the keys. The writer wrote the images, and the director responded.

So you can tell the story visually without directing the camera, and that's what you should do.

Novelist wannabes

Many writers are "too good" for screenwriting, or so they think. That is, they are too much in love with rich, flowery prose for the crisp, lean rhetoric of screenwriting. The screenplay should not be regarded as a literary form to be read so much as a blueprint for a movie and a business proposal for a very expensive collaboration.

The trend in screenwriting rhetoric has been toward leaner and crisper writing, and if you are in love with language so much that you think ten words are better than one word any time, then screenwriting is probably not for you.

What happened to the main character?

In many student scripts, somewhere in the middle the main character gets lost. Some other character becomes more interesting and begins to carry the story. Maybe it's the Opponent, or a friend (ally) of the main character, but the main character disappears for pages and pages. This is a clear red flag that something has gone wrong with the focus of the story.

One of the reasons I like screenwriting software (besides ease of format) is for the reports they generate. I like to look at these reports and see how many pages of script I have without the presence of the protagonist. More than three, and I double-check focus because that much time away from the main character worries me.

Think of your main character as played by a superstar with a huge ego. Every moment the superstar is not on screen is a moment you must defend. You will find yourself doing this as infrequently as possible.

In other words, since your story is about the main character, he should be on screen as often as possible.

Stay focused. Who is your main character, what is his or her goal, and what is stopping success of reaching it? These are the immediate questions we need answered to understand your story. You need to address them sooner rather than later. Poor focus on the main character is a common error I see. Keep your main character on screen as much as possible, even two or three pages off the screen may be enough to knock the story focus askew. Keep on the main character like glue.

In my classes, I try to get students to solve the rhetorical challenges of screenwriting (fiction writing, slow dialogue) as soon as possible so they can concentrate on the story issues like focus. Screenwriting, in fact, is more about storytelling than writing as we usually think about it. Yet the rhetorical issues occupy some students for most of the term, as if they have a hard time accepting that screenwriting is not literary writing. Some have observed a trend in screenwriting to greater literary quality (*The Hours* script comes to mind), but it must be remembered that these examples are written by established writers. The plight of the spec script writer is different and much more competitive. To be read in such an environment requires special attention to economy so that your story is easily found and understood.

Screenwriting is the only form of writing about which it can be said: don't let your writing get in the way of your story. Keep it simple. Keep it clear. Keep it focused.

<u>Is this all there is?</u>

What does your story add up to? What has changed in the life of the main character as a result of experiencing the story? And what does the audience walk out of the theater with?

Movies are bigger than life. Many beginning screenwriters are too concerned about "being real" to understand that movies actually are not real: they are bigger than life. That's why we go to them!

So a lot of student scripts get this comment from me: "Crank it up!" Make it larger, more consequential, make it matter more to the hero and to us. Make the stakes bigger, the threats bigger, the payoff bigger. Crank it up.

Movies are bigger than life. Never forget that, and tell your story accordingly.

These are some of the common mistakes my students make over and over again. In my first draft, I still make a lot of them myself. It's okay to make them, as long as we rewrite to correct them. Writing is a process, and the key to this process is being able to recognize your own mistakes so you can go back and correct them.

Less is More

When in doubt, leave it out! Less is more.

Let's look at how to put the philosophy of "less is more" into practice when revising the draft of a screenplay. I'll focus on two areas where my screenwriting students do most of their over-writing: in dialogue and in description.

Less Dialogue

Often you can tell at first glance if a scene has a dialogue problem. This is when a series of long speeches are exchanged, each consistently taking up more than several lines in the block of dialogue text, one character speaking for a dozen lines, another answering for a dozen or so more, and so on, large blocks of dialogue text filling the page.

When I see this problem in a student script, after checking that in fact the exchange is much too verbose, becoming repetitive and therefore boring, I often copy the pages in order to do a classroom exercise. I pass out the scene as originally written, select students to read the parts, and direct a staged reading. We discuss it. Scenes based on large exchanges of dialogue are almost always painfully slow, and the class quickly picks up on this. They identify the common moments of repetition that happen in such scenes.

Then I take out my red pen and very dramatically start crossing out lines. Over the years I've learned that most fat in a long speech comes in the middle. So I typically might cross out, in a 12-line speech, lines 3 through 11, leaving the first, second and last—and that's all. Perhaps I have to add a phrase to make for a smooth transition.

I continue this through the entire scene, crossing out half to two-thirds of the dialogue. Then we replay the scene. The improvement is astounding! The pace immediately quickens because now the exchanges are quick and snappy, not long and verbose. There is no repetition to cause boredom.

The class looks at me as if I'm a magician, able to fix a scene so dramatically by doing nothing more than hacking out excess lines of dialogue. I'm not a magician. I have experience. I've read many thousands of pages of verbose, over-written dialogue. Often I can spot it half a room away.

The key test to any line of dialogue in a script is this: what is lost if it is removed? If precious little is lost, then cut it. Every line of dialogue needs to move the story forward in a fresh way or make a point about character that we don't already know. Verbosity is your enemy. Less is more.

Less Description

Here is the description of Nash's fantasy CIA connection in *A Beautiful Mind*: "Fine dark suit. Thin tie. WILLIAM PARCHER." This is all the character description we get!

Here is how we meet the title character in *Citizen Ruth*: "She is around 30." No more.

Clarice Starling in *Silence of the Lambs*: "Trim, very pretty, mid-20s." That's it. The antagonist, however, gets more detail because he is more unusual: "A face so long out of the sun, it seems almost leached—except for the glittering eyes, and the wet red mouth."

Descriptions of place get no more detail than descriptions of character.

From *The Ice Storm*: "A large New England Colonial, with a few modern additions and touches."

From *Good Will Hunting*: "The bar is dirty, more than a little run down."

Neither of these comes close to the long, verbose descriptions of character and place that my students love to write, especially those who come from a background in fiction. None of this detail is appropriate in a screenplay. Understand this and you will solve your tendency to over-write description.

The screenwriter is a collaborator. He or she is not the costume designer. He or she is not the set designer. A screenwriter writes a "fine dark suit" and lets the costume designer pick the color, writes "a thin tie" and lets the costume designer select the details. A screenwriter writes "stuffed animals everywhere and posters of pop idols," letting the set designer select *which animals* and *which pop idols* belong on the set.

Write with an awareness that you are a collaborator. Write so it doesn't sound like you are telling the costume designer and the set designer how to do their jobs. Your job is to give them the appropriate clues so they can do their job in a way consistent with the context of the story.

The Writing and the Story

A screenplay is a blueprint for a movie. It should be written accordingly, lean and mean, in a style that lets the story flow quickly, vertically, down the page. Your job is not to let the writing get in the way of the story.

Think about that. What an odd thing to tell a writer! Don't let the writing get in the way of the story. We are used to thinking about "writing" the way a novelist thinks about it, as the every essence of the story, literary style being everything. Screenwriting style is more subtle and more poetic because there are far less literary tools to use.

When beginning screenwriters over-write, they let their writing get in the way of the story. Excess verbiage becomes camouflage, hiding story movement, and becomes misdirection from the spine of the story, which needs to be abundantly clear, quickly, and throughout the script.

Don't let this happen in your script. Make your writing serve your story because a producer isn't going to buy your writing, he or she's going to buy your *story.*

Not everything about screenwriting can be taught, including what may be the most important thing from a commercial perspective, story concept. Producers buy stories, not writing. A screenplay is a blueprint for a movie (not a literary document) and is not read for pleasure, like a novel, so much as for practical reasons: Is the script we are looking for as the basis of a movie we are willing to spend millions of dollars to make? The story is king.

No one has ever figured out how to teach students to create dynamite story concepts. Oh, sure, you can look at successful film stories and make generalizations about them. This is Monday morning quarterbacking. Coming up with story concepts that start bidding wars, that are seen as instant "necessary movies," is quite another matter. So while I can teach students how to structure their stories in a more powerful way and how to write the scripts with economy so the writing doesn't camouflage the story, I can't teach anyone how to come up with a great idea. If I could, I'd be a millionaire.

There is actually something that can be taught and it is taught within these pages in detail, Structure.

NOTES

0-595-34627-8

CPSIA information can be obtained at www.ICGtesting.com
Printed in the USA
BVOW06s0125260214

346051BV00001B/2/P

9 780595 346271